Dolores Huerta

VOICE FOR THE WORKING POOR

By Alex Van Tol

Crabtree Publishing Company
www.crabtreebooks.com

Crabtree Publishing Company

www.crabtreebooks.com

Author: Alex Van Tol
Publishing plan research and development:
Sean Charlebois, Reagan Miller
Crabtree Publishing Company
Editors: Mark Sachner, Lynn Peppas
Proofreader: Wendy Scavuzzo
Indexer: Wendy Scavuzzo
Editorial director: Kathy Middleton
Photo researcher: Ruth Owen
Designer: Alix Wood
Production coordinator: Margaret Amy Salter
Production: Kim Richardson
Prepress technician: Margaret Amy Salter

Written, developed, and produced by
Water Buffalo Books

Publisher's note:
All quotations in this book come from original sources and contain the spelling and grammatical inconsistencies of the original text. The use of such constructions is for the sake of preserving the historical and literary accuracy of the sources.

Photographs and reproductions:
Favianna.com: page 20; page 38; page 39; page 51; page 60; page 79; page 91; page 101
Flickr (Creative Commons): front cover (main); page 1; page 4 (inset); page 5; page 13; page 27; page 41; page 53; page 67; page 85; page 95; page 97; page 103 Getty Images: John W. Keith: page 7; Cathy Murphy: page 15; Cathy Murphy: page 31; Arthur Schatz: page 36; Arthur Schatz: page 43; Arthur Schatz: page 55; Cathy Murphy: page 59; Cathy Murphy: page 69; page 71; Barbara Freeman: page 73; Cathy Murphy: page 77; Cathy Murphy: page 83
Library of Congress: page 16; page 17; page 22 (all); page 23; page 35; page 48; page 50; page 62; page 70; page 78
Shutterstock: front cover (background); page 4 (background); page 11; page 18; page 19; page 24; page 25; page 29; page 32; page 65; page 68; page 74; page 87; page 88; page 90
Wikipedia (public domain): page 47 (top); page 47 (bottom); page 71; page 93

Cover: Dolores Huerta was no stranger to the farm workers' plight. Her father had worked in the fields and her mother gave poor farm workers a place to stay at her hotel. Although Dolores began her career as a schoolteacher, she quickly realized she could make more of a difference in the lives of the children by helping their farm-worker families earn fair wages and improve their living conditions.

Library and Archives Canada Cataloguing in Publication

Van Tol, Alex
Dolores Huerta : voice for the working poor / Alex Van Tol.

(Crabtree groundbreaker biographies)
Includes index.
Issued also in an electronic format.
ISBN 978-0-7787-2536-7 (bound).--ISBN 978-0-7787-2545-9 (pbk.)

1. Huerta, Dolores, 1930- --Juvenile literature. 2. Mexican American women labor leaders--Biography--Juvenile literature. 3. Women social reformers--United States--Biography--Juvenile literature. 4. Labor leaders--Biography--Juvenile literature. 5. Social reformers--United States--Biography--Juvenile literature. I. Title. II. Series: Crabtree groundbreaker biographies

HD6509.H84V35 2011   j331.88'13092   C2010-903024-9

Library of Congress Cataloging-in-Publication Data

Van Tol, Alex.
Dolores Huerta : voice for the working poor / Alex Van Tol.
p. cm. -- (Crabtree groundbreaker biographies)
Includes index.
ISBN 978-0-7787-2545-9 (pbk. : alk. paper) --
ISBN 978-0-7787-2536-7 (reinforced library binding : alk. paper) -- ISBN 978-1-4271-9468-8 (electronic (pdf))
1. Huerta, Dolores, 1930---Juvenile literature. 2. Women labor leaders--United States--Biography--Juvenile literature. 3. Mexican American women labor union members--Biography--Juvenile literature. 4. Mexican American migrant agricultural laborers--Labor unions--Organizing--History--Juvenile literature. I. Title. II. Series.

HD6509.H84V36 2011
331.88'13092--dc22
[B]
                                        2010018044

Crabtree Publishing Company

www.crabtreebooks.com   1-800-387-7650

Printed in the USA/082010/BL20100723

Published in Canada
Crabtree Publishing
616 Welland Ave.
St. Catharines, Ontario
L2M 5V6

Published in the United States
Crabtree Publishing
PMB 59051
350 Fifth Avenue, 59th Floor
New York, New York 10118

Published in the United Kingdom
Crabtree Publishing
Maritime House
Basin Road North, Hove
BN41 1WR

Published in Australia
Crabtree Publishing
386 Mt. Alexander Rd.
Ascot Vale (Melbourne)
VIC 3032

Contents

Chapter 1
Elementary Teacher Turned Activist

In the early 1950s, Dolores Huerta was the kind of schoolteacher kids loved. She was young, pretty, smart, and full of energy. Above all else, she liked spending time with her students. She looked forward to making the classroom a safe place for them. Just a few months into her teaching assignment, however, Dolores realized the job was all wrong for her:

"I couldn't stand seeing kids come to class hungry and needing shoes. I thought I could do more by organizing farm workers than by trying to teach their hungry children."

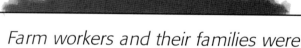

Farm workers and their families were very poor. They almost always lived below the poverty level.

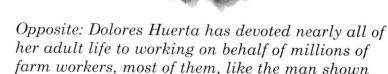

Opposite: Dolores Huerta has devoted nearly all of her adult life to working on behalf of millions of farm workers, most of them, like the man shown here, of Mexican descent.

Tough Luck: Life as a Migrant Farm Worker

It wasn't an easy job. Farm workers were often mistreated. They received little thanks from growers or even the public. In the 1950s and early 1960s, farm workers made very low wages—between 75 cents and a dollar per hour. Sometimes they made a little bit of extra money for every bushel or basket of whatever item they were picking. In 1965, for example, grape pickers made about 90 cents per hour. They got two extra pennies for every full

Kids of farm workers never stayed long enough in one place to form lasting friendships. Sometimes the kids had to miss school and join their parents working in the fields.

basket of grapes they picked. Farm workers and their families were very poor. They almost always lived below the poverty level.

There were state laws in place that set out how employers were supposed to treat their farm workers. Most farm and ranch owners paid no attention to these rules. Conditions at the farms were terrible and left no room for human dignity.

In this photo, taken in the mid-1950s, a Mexican man and woman harvest onions on a farm in California with the help of their four young boys. Although child labor was against the law, families needed to make money to eat, and this often meant keeping their kids with them and even putting them to work.

WHO WERE THE MIGRANT FARM WORKERS?

In 1965, about 466,000 migrant farm workers lived in the United States. They came from many different ethnic backgrounds. There were whites, Asians, Hispanics, and African-Americans. Their numbers included immigrants and U.S. citizens alike. In California, most of the farm workers were from Mexico. They had first started crossing Mexico's northern border into California in 1848.

Whether they were white or members of a visible minority, migrant farm workers were treated poorly. People did not show them much respect.

At one farm, all the workers had to drink from the same cup—an empty beer can. They worked under the sun all day. In the hot fields, temperatures would sometimes soar to higher than 100 °F (about 38 °C). At another farm, the workers were forced to pay 25 cents every time they wanted to have a drink! There were no portable toilets for workers to use. They were forced to live in metal shacks with no heat. These crude shelters had no indoor plumbing or kitchens. Often the workers had to pay two dollars a day to be allowed to live in these terrible conditions.

Workers were exposed to poisonous pesticides every day. They were not offered masks. They weren't given suits to keep them safe from the toxic fumes, either.

Farm workers and their families traveled around a lot. They had to go wherever there was work. They constantly drove around the crop-growing regions looking for fruit and vegetables to pick. Their children were bounced around from school to school. Kids of farm workers never stayed long enough in one place to form lasting friendships. Sometimes the kids had to miss school and join their parents working in the fields. Even though child labor was against the law, they had to work. It was the only way the family could afford to eat.

In the winter, farm workers would pick the crops in southern Florida, southern Texas, or central California. When summer came around, they'd pack their cars and head north. They would spend the summer picking crops at higher latitudes.

Farm families had to suffer periods of extreme poverty. Sometimes there was no work due to the changing seasons. Sometimes the weather prevented them from picking and, if their car broke down, they would have trouble getting to a different spot to keep working.

Migrant farm workers couldn't rely on their jobs to be stable. Their work ended when the crop was brought in, and so they had little job security. If a farm owner was unhappy with a picker for any reason, he or she would simply be fired.

Workers were exposed to poisonous pesticides every day. They were not offered masks. They weren't given suits to keep them safe from the toxic fumes, either. In the 1950s, health insurance didn't exist for farm workers. There were no retirement funds or social security or welfare benefits. Accidents in the fields happened three times more often than they did in other lines of work. If a fruit picker got hurt, his family had to hope he would recover quickly. They needed him to be able to work! Many workers were injured or died from accidents on the job. Diseases like tuberculosis and pneumonia hit migrant farm workers harder and more often than they did other

Americans. Babies born to migrant farm workers were twice as likely to die as babies in the general U.S. population. In 1960, a farm worker could expect to live for about 49 years. The average American could expect to live to age 68. That's a difference of almost 20 years!

Being a farm worker meant three things: hard work, little pay, and unfair treatment by farm owners.

Working for the Children

Dolores was no stranger to the farm worker's lifestyle. Her father had worked in the fields when she was a little girl. When Dolores was a bit older, her mother took in farm workers and gave them a place to stay. Dolores understood that farm work was hard.

Dolores wanted to do good work that made a difference to people. Her first career was as a teacher in Stockton. The city lay deep in the heart of northern California's fertile agricultural lands. The area was home to many migrant farm workers. It broke Dolores's heart a little each day to see the children of farm workers coming to school without shoes or lunches. She spent much of her time trying to find extra shoes, milk, and food for these children whose parents were so desperately poor.

That's when she knew something had to change.

Doesn't Anyone Else Care?

The principal at the elementary school told Dolores to forget about it. He said there was no use in trying to help the children. He told her

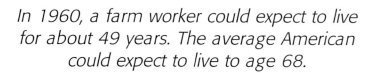

In 1960, a farm worker could expect to live for about 49 years. The average American could expect to live to age 68.

their parents were drunks who spent all their money on booze, leaving nothing for clothes or food. Dolores was shocked to realize that he just didn't care. Neither did the other teachers.

Dolores took extra yard duty outside at recess so she could be with the children of these poor families. She felt as if she belonged with them. She didn't feel as if she belonged in the staff room. That's where the other teachers sat around and talked about their vacations and new cars. Dolores was deeply saddened that the teachers didn't want to do more to help these kids. She was angry with the principal for saying the children's parents were lazy drunks. She knew their families worked hard all day long. She also knew they loved their children but couldn't provide for them because they were paid such low wages.

Dolores wanted to help the migrant farm workers. She realized it wasn't enough to simply try to teach their hungry children. She'd have to work against poverty in a more direct manner.

Little did she know at the time that she would devote every year of her life after that to the cause.

Chapter 2
The Fighting Spirit Runs in the Family

Dolores Huerta was born Dolores Fernandez in the town of Dawson, New Mexico, on April 10, 1930. It was a small mining town in the New Mexico mountains. Her father, Juan Fernandez, the son of Mexican immigrants, was a farm worker and miner. Dolores's mother was Alicia Chaves Fernandez. Her heritage was Hispanic, but her family had lived in New Mexico for a number of generations. Dolores had an older brother, John, and a younger brother, Marshall.

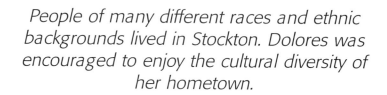

People of many different races and ethnic backgrounds lived in Stockton. Dolores was encouraged to enjoy the cultural diversity of her hometown.

Moving to Stockton

Young Dolores wasn't destined to have a perfect two-parent family. Her parents divorced in the mid-1930s. She and her two brothers moved with their mother away from New Mexico. They eventually settled in Stockton, in California's San Joaquin Valley. People of many different races and ethnic backgrounds lived in Stockton. Dolores was encouraged to enjoy the cultural diversity of her hometown.

The San Joaquin Valley

The San Joaquin Valley is located in central California. It's sometimes called "the nation's salad bowl." It occupies the southern part of California's much larger Central Valley. At the northern end of the Central Valley is the Sacramento Valley. The Sacramento Valley gets a lot of annual rainfall, but the San Joaquin Valley is hot and dry in the summertime. In some places, it's almost like a desert. Stockton is one of the larger cities in the valley. Bakersfield, Sacramento, and Fresno are a few others.

The valley produces a huge variety of vegetable and fruit crops—almost 13 percent of the total value of U.S. agricultural production! Grapes, almonds, pistachios, asparagus, and citrus fruits grow here. The valley is also home to many cattle and dairy farms, as well as the world's largest cotton farm.

The San Joaquin Valley is also a large producer of oil and gas. Small oil wells dot the valley. This is where the third-largest oil field in the United States is located.

Dolores Huerta is shown at a labor rally in Calexico, California, in the mid-1970s. Dolores became familiar with the plight of migrant farm workers as a girl growing up in the 1930s and 1940s. In the 1950s, she set out on the path that would lead her to become a prominent labor activist and co-founder of the United Farm Workers of America.

Until about five million years ago, the San Joaquin Valley was submerged under the ocean. The valley started to form when the coastal mountains were slowly pushed up by the gradual shifting of the Earth's crust. About two million years ago, huge glaciers moved into the valley. They advanced and retreated over several different ice ages. As they did, they left behind huge freshwater lakes. Until about

She was glad to have been raised by a fair-minded mother who treated her as an equal to her brothers.

700,000 years ago, the floor of the San Joaquin Valley was entirely covered by a huge lake! Over all those years, rich sediments were deposited at the bottom of the lakebed. This is what makes the land so fertile today.

In recent years, the area was covered by natural grasslands. Nearly all of those have now been lost to farming. Very little of the San Joaquin Valley's land remains in a natural state. Over the past 20 years, people have built more and more homes in the region. Experts are worried about what will become of the San Joaquin Valley's agricultural lands if cities keep growing this way.

Just as when Dolores was young, the San Joaquin Valley is still home to many poor

THE CHANGING FACES OF MIGRANT FARM WORKERS

The San Joaquin Valley is home to people of many different ethnic and racial backgrounds. Most of the farmers and rich landowners throughout its history have been white. During Dolores's growing-up years in Stockton, she shared the valley with people of Mexican, Portuguese, Yugoslav, Dutch, Sikh, Pakistani, Swedish, and Armenian descent.

Not long after Dolores was born, a large number of farm families began arriving. They had been displaced from states east of California, such as Arkansas, Texas, Kansas, and Oklahoma. Years of drought had dried up the land that their families had farmed for generations. They could no longer farm.

Later, during the 1970s and 1980s, many Hmong, Cambodian, Vietnamese, and Laotian immigrants began arriving. They came after the Vietnam War. These ethnic Asian groups settled in the larger cities of the valley.

Migrant children sit on top of family belongings piled on the back of a truck in the San Joaquin Valley. In the 1930s, thousands of families, desperate for work harvesting the crops of California, traveled and lived like this. This picture was taken by Dorothea Lange, famed for her photos of people living in the 1930s' era of economic hardship known as the Great Depression.

Mechanized harvesting equipment in this carrot field contribute smoke and other pollutants that collect to form smog in the San Joaquin Valley.

people. Many of them are among the poorest in all of the United States.

Growing Up in Stockton

In Stockton, Dolores's mother, Alicia, worked in a cannery by night and as a waitress during the daytime. Within a few years, she had saved enough of her money to buy a small restaurant. Alicia eventually remarried. She had another daughter with her husband, James Richards. The couple bought a hotel in a working-class section of town. All the siblings worked together to help their mother run the hotel.

It was a successful family business. Dolores's years working there helped teach her about the value of hard work. She was glad to have been raised by a fair-minded mother who treated her as an equal to her brothers. Instead of doing the cooking and washing like so many other girl children of Mexican families, Dolores and her brothers were given the same chores—and the same status.

The marriage between Alicia and James Richards did not last long. Alicia married Juan Silva a short time later, and the couple had another daughter.

A Strong Mother Sets a Good Example

Alicia Fernandez's hotel had 70 rooms. She was a hardworking, independent

THE SMOG OF THE SAN JOAQUIN

People worry about the air quality in the San Joaquin Valley. Pollution is created every day by valley farm operations. Just think of all the tractors, factories, and big trucks at work in the valley on any given day! That's a lot of fossil fuel emissions. Cattle also release methane gas, which adds to the air-quality problem.

The San Joaquin Valley is a low-lying land formation. This means that smoke and other pollutants tend to collect in a haze known as smog. There's not much wind to blow the smog around, either. Air quality in the San Joaquin Valley is sometimes almost as bad as it is in Los Angeles. Some days people are advised to stay inside to avoid breathing the polluted air.

Combines harvest corn in California's San Joaquin Valley.

businesswoman—but she had a heart filled with compassion. She often took in farm worker families for a low rate. Sometimes she even let them stay for free. She recognized that these families needed every penny they earned. "My mother was very quiet," Dolores recalled, "and she was very effective at whatever she did, and very ambitious."

Alicia taught her children to be generous and respectful of everyone, regardless of race or class. Dolores's mother also taught her to care for others. Dolores learned to appreciate all different kinds of people during her years working in the hotel.

Alicia was an active participant in her community. She was involved in the church and other community organizations. She set an example for her daughter to be involved and outspoken. Alicia served as a positive influence for Dolores throughout her life. Dolores and her siblings were raised as devout Catholics. Their mother believed in the importance of the morals and values of the church. In high school, Dolores was popular and a good student. She was fully bilingual in Spanish and English.

For a while, Dolores yearned to be a Flamenco dancer when she grew up!

¡VIVA DOLORES!

The Pain of Discrimination

The period of economic hardship during the 1930s known as the Great Depression and the years of World War II during the 1940s were a tough time to grow up. It was especially hard for a kid who wasn't white. Dolores often felt discriminated against because of her Mexican heritage.

An Inspiring Father Figure

Dolores did not see her father, Juan Fernandez, often because her parents had divorced when she was a toddler. When she was a little girl, he added farm work to his coal-mining income. He traveled around with other migrant workers. They harvested beets in Nebraska, Wyoming, and Colorado. Juan experienced the poor working conditions of the job. He made low wages. He saw people have accidents. The injustices in the fields made him angry. This is when he first became interested in labor issues.

Juan Fernandez took a union leadership position. He began to speak up for workers' rights. He worked as the secretary-treasurer of the Congress of Industrial Organizations at the Terrero Camp of the American Metals Company in Las Vegas. His union experience later helped him get elected to the New Mexico state legislature in 1938. He pushed for changes to pass a labor program. He demanded legislation to raise wages and help farm workers improve their working conditions.

When Dolores grew up, she got back in touch with Juan. He eventually returned to school and earned his bachelor's degree. Dolores was proud of his political successes and his commitment to union activism. Though he never fully supported her decision to put her career ahead of her family, Juan did support Dolores's union organizing later in her life.

Dolores and her father had a cordial relationship until his death. He served as an inspiration to Dolores in her own career as a labor activist.

Dolores of the Seven Tongues

It was tough for the young family to make a go of it in those first years after arriving from New Mexico. Alicia Chaves Fernandez leaned on her extended family for support. Dolores was lucky to grow up surrounded by her cousins, aunts, and uncles. She was especially close to her grandfather. He looked after Dolores and her siblings while her mother was at work. He teasingly called her "seven tongues" because she liked to talk so much.

Dolores adored her grandfather. "My grandfather kind of raised us," she said in an interview many years later. "He was really our father ... [His] influence was really the male influence in my family."

Jobs were hard to come by in the 1930s. Many U.S. citizens were angry at the idea of migrant farm workers "stealing" jobs away from Americans. The U.S. government actually rounded up large numbers of migrant workers and sent them back to Mexico.

At school, Dolores felt the sting of racism. Her teachers treated her differently than they treated white students. She won a Girl Scout essay contest, but school officials didn't let her take the trip to a nearby Hopi Indian reservation that was the prize for having won. Dolores was angry about this. All the white kids who had won the contest in previous years had been allowed to go.

Above: A "squatter" camp of migrants set up on a road near Calipatria, California, during the early 1930s. Forty families camped, or squatted, for months hoping for work in the nearby pea fields. They were fleeing from the Dust Bowl—an area in parts of the southwest and Great Plains in North American that had suffered severe drought due to dust storms, windstorms, and soil erosion at that time. The pea crop was frozen, however, and so there was no work for them.

Abandoned machinery in South Dakota. This farm has been laid bare by windstorms and soil erosion, and buried under tons of sand and dirt carried by sandstorms. This was the Dust Bowl, which brought ecological and economic disaster to parts of North America in the 1930s.

THE GREAT DEPRESSION

The Great Depression began around 1929 and stretched through the 1930s. It was an economic downturn that sent shock waves across the world. Some experts say the Great Depression began with the U.S. stock market crash of 1929. People and companies lost millions of dollars. Others say the crash happened because the depression was already underway. Either way, the outcome was bad. Trade between countries collapsed, which affected jobs. People's incomes went down or completely disappeared. Governments couldn't collect enough taxes. Unemployment rose to as high as 25 percent in the United States—even higher in some countries.

Crop prices plunged by about 60 percent. Terrible weather conditions made matters even worse. Severe drought dried up farmland across the country. Between 1930 and 1936, severe windstorms swept away the farmers' soil. Millions of acres of agricultural land sat useless. Five hundred thousand people were forced to leave their homes. Most of them were farm families. They traveled to other states, where they lived as poor migrant workers.

Dolores started a teen center so kids could get together and listen to music, dance, and play games. It was eventually closed down because officials didn't want to see whites mixing with Filipino, Mexican, and African American kids. Dolores sold more war bonds than any of her friends, but she was never given the reward that had been promised. This kind of discrimination was a shock to a kid who had always treated everyone equally.

Higher Education

Dolores had always planned to continue her education by attending college. She enrolled in Delta Community College at the University of the Pacific. Dolores was the first person in the family to even attend college. Her mother was very proud of her. Not many Hispanic girls of Dolores's day and age went to college after high school. Neither, for that matter, did many Hispanic boys.

In 1950, Dolores met and married her first husband, Ralph Head. He had been her high school sweetheart. She took some time off from school to have two

"My mother was always pushing me to get involved in all these youth activities. We took violin lessons. I took piano lessons. I took dancing lessons. I belonged to the church choir … I belonged to the church youth organization. And I was a very active Girl Scout from the time I was eight to the time I was 18."

Dolores reflecting on how active a child her mother encouraged her to be.

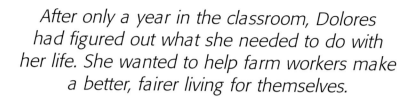

After only a year in the classroom, Dolores had figured out what she needed to do with her life. She wanted to help farm workers make a better, fairer living for themselves.

daughters with Ralph: Celeste and Lori. She worked at a grocery store and as a secretary, and even worked in the sheriff's office for a while. Her marriage to Ralph Head only lasted until 1953. Dolores decided she wasn't happy working at any of the jobs she had, so she decided to finish her college studies.

Leaving her daughters in her mother's care, Dolores returned to school. There, she earned an associate degree with a certificate in teaching. Dolores was eager to make a positive impact on the lives of others as an educator. After only a year in the classroom, however, Dolores had figured out what she needed to do with her life. She wanted to help farm workers make a better, fairer living for themselves. She reasoned that she would be able to do better work by helping her students' parents get higher wages and helping improve their lives in other ways.

Chapter 3
The Irresistible Pull of Social Activism

A wave of civic activism was sweeping the nation in the wake of World War II. It swept through the Mexican-American community, too—and Dolores jumped right in. She helped start the Stockton chapter of the Community Service Organization (CSO) in 1955. Her mother and one of her aunts joined up, as well.

Serving with the Stockton CSO

Dolores had heard about the great things CSO could do. Fred Ross, the CSO's main organizer, was working at the CSO's Los Angeles headquarters. He believed that the CSO was the perfect fit for a spunky young woman like Dolores. Ross knew she wanted to make a difference for the farm workers in her community. At the Stockton CSO, Dolores

He believed that the CSO was the perfect fit for a spunky young woman like Dolores.

discovered her dream job as an organizer.

The CSO was an organization that brought people together to try to improve their social, economic, and political conditions. The CSO aimed to help Mexican, Filipino, African-American, Japanese, and Chinese working families living in Stockton. The CSO tried to get people to be more politically active. It helped people learn how to vote and take part in public decision making.

Nearly all the farm workers in the San Joaquin Valley are people of Mexican heritage. The CSO fought segregation and pushed for better public services, such as streetlights and parks. Dolores and other CSO workers pressed for improvements to the *barrios* (Spanish-speaking neighborhoods). They wanted to see better streets and playgrounds. They led classes to prepare immigrants for applying to get their U.S. citizenship.

Dolores and her fellow CSO workers helped people register to vote who wouldn't have been able to do it themselves. She fought to have the rules changed so that non-citizens could have access to things like welfare and other public assistance programs.

Dolores decided, however, that she cared more about helping other people than about cleaning her house and styling her hair.

During her years working at the CSO, Dolores met a man who was also interested in community affairs. His name was Ventura Huerta. The two married and had five children: Fidel, Emilio, Vincent, Alicia, and Angela.

Ventura Huerta was Dolores's second husband. Their marriage ended in divorce after several years. Ventura didn't approve of Dolores's commitment to political activism. It made her life too busy. He wanted her to stay at home with the children. Dolores decided, however, that she cared more about helping other people than about cleaning her house and styling her hair. She stuck to her beliefs. She insisted to Ventura that she wanted to work at making society better instead.

The divorce was bitter but, again, Dolores was able to lean on her mother for emotional and financial support. Alicia helped watch the children so Dolores could keep doing what she loved best: helping farm workers.

Victories at the CSO

In 1958, Dolores and several other CSO supporters set up the Agricultural Workers Association (AWA). The AWA still operated within the CSO. While the CSO mostly helped Mexican-Americans living in the cities, the AWA dealt with the specific concerns facing farm workers. Poverty and exploitation by their employers were big problems for farm laborers. It was important to Dolores that there was an arm of the CSO that looked out for the farm workers and their families.

During her time at the CSO, Dolores pushed for changes to legislation. She demanded that

FRED ROSS, FATHER OF THE CSO

Fred Ross had been trained as a teacher. When, in the 1930s, the worldwide financial crisis known as the Great Depression devastated the nation's economy, he was unable to find work in the classroom. After working for about a year as a government social worker, he quit and took a job with the Farm Security Administration. This was a government-led effort to help farmers who had been displaced by the drought caused by the ecological catastrophe known as the Dust Bowl. The idea was that these farmers would work together to farm land owned by the government. Ross supervised labor camps in Arizona and California. He was deeply troubled by the poverty and poor working conditions of the people. That's when he decided to devote his energies toward organizing people. He wanted to gather poor workers together and help them stand up for their rights.

Just before the end of World War II, 38-year-old Fred Ross founded the Community Service Organization (CSO) with help from several Mexican-Americans. The year was 1948. His goal was to help Mexican-Americans who were living in California. He wanted to get these people together so they could discuss issues that were important to them, and look for ways to change their situation.

Community organizer Fred Ross stands next to Dolores Huerta at a press conference in Livingston, California, in the mid-1970s. As founder of the Community Service Organization (CSO), Ross had an early influence on Dolores's career as a labor activist. In this photo, Ross and Huerta are shown supporting a boycott of grapes and wines produced by growers and companies exploiting farm workers.

voters have the right to vote in Spanish. She asked for government to allow people to take their drivers' license test in their native language. She lobbied the California government to let farm workers participate in pension programs.

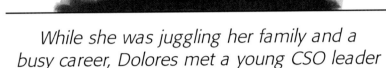

While she was juggling her family and a busy career, Dolores met a young CSO leader named César Chávez.

Meeting César Chávez

While she was juggling her family and a busy career, Dolores met a young CSO leader named César Chávez. He, too, was interested in the problems of migrant farm workers.

When Dolores first met César Chávez, he was working in Los Angeles at the CSO headquarters. He was its general director. At the time, Dolores didn't think César was much of a leader. He seemed shy and quiet, and his modest physical size was anything but inspiring. He was so different from her! Yet, even then, he already had gained a reputation as being really good at organizing people.

Dolores showed a particular talent for lobbying government at the local level. Before long, the CSO recognized her abilities and asked her to represent its interests at the state level. To be invited to be a lobbyist for the organization was a huge achievement! Until then, only men had been permitted to hold the position, but César had seen something unique in Dolores. He knew she was going to be a great advantage to the CSO. She carried herself well, spoke clearly and forcefully, and didn't like to back down. She was perfect for the job.

César and Dolores were united in their concern for the welfare of farm workers. They worked to bring their ideas to the CSO's attention. The pair wanted to launch a CSO campaign to organize the migrant laborers. They wanted to create a union so that the farm workers' voices would be heard. Acting together as a union, the farm workers would be able to demand higher wages and better working conditions from their employers.

The CSO was worried about wading into a fight on behalf of such an unpopular group. After all, some of the workers didn't even belong in the United States. They were working there illegally. Besides, trying to unite a constantly moving group of people was difficult. They were uneducated and didn't speak English. And they wanted to take on the giant farming companies? It was more than the CSO wanted to deal with.

In the end, the CSO didn't want to get involved. César and Dolores were deeply disappointed.

In 1961, César Chávez had had enough. He was irritated that he couldn't push the CSO to help unionize farm workers. He called Dolores

THE BRACERO PROGRAM

In 1942, the U.S. and Mexican governments decided to work together to bring temporary workers from Mexico to the United States. This was called the Bracero Program. (*Bracero* comes from *brazo,* the Spanish word for "arm.") It worked well because each side needed the other's help. The United States needed workers because the World War II effort had called away so many Americans. The Mexicans needed to earn wages. The Bracero Program first began by bringing workers to the Stockton, California, area. Soon after, workers spread to other parts of the United States to work in the fields.

The original agreement ended in 1947. Farmers realized, however, that they still needed help in their fields. Both governments agreed that agricultural workers would continue to cross the border to work in the United States. The Bracero Program continued for many more years.

Braceros were cheap for farmers to hire. They cost less than workers who belonged to a union. When there were strikes, farmers brought in braceros to work in the fields. Sometimes this would be enough to break the strike and force the unionized workers back to their jobs.

Braceros were a good thing for growers to have handy. Since they would work for low pay, large-scale growers knew their crops wouldn't rot in the fields—even if there was a strike. Growers demanded that the Bracero Program continue, and the government allowed it.

The Bracero Program continued until 1964. It was brought to an end when religious, ethnic, and labor groups applied pressure to the government to stop the program.

Although laws exist today restricting how or when Mexicans can enter the United States, many of these laws are ignored. The U.S.-Mexican border is easily crossed in many places. The law is often not enforced. Many Mexicans, believing they will find a better life for themselves in the United States, continue to slip across the border. It doesn't usually turn out well. Discrimination against Mexican arrivals is strong. Growers know they'll still work for next to nothing, so they don't end up making very good wages. Coming to the United States doesn't always turn out to be such a dream, after all.

Mexican workers await legal employment in the United States in February 1954. These workers are in the United States under the rules of the Bracero Program, which began in World War II to help fill jobs left vacant by Americans who were in the armed forces. Over the years, the large commercial growers took unfair advantage of the cheap labor they were able to obtain by hiring braceros, and the program was discontinued in 1964.

United Farm Workers leader César Chávez poses in 1968 with pictures of Robert F. Kennedy (left) and Mohandas Gandhi in the background. Gandhi inspired much of Chávez's thinking, and Kennedy was a political ally until his death in 1968.

to his home. "We have got to start the union," he said. "If we don't do it, nobody else will."

Chávez the Charismatic

César was in his early 30s when he first met Dolores Huerta. Born in 1927, he was the son of migrant farm workers. His father had been cheated out of the family home in Arizona by an unfair Anglo landowner. After leaving Arizona, César's family moved to California. They worked in farmers' fields all over the state. His family lived in the roughest barrios.

César spoke only Spanish at home, so he

GANDHI: THE MAN WHO GUIDED CHÁVEZ

Born in India in 1869, Mohandas Gandhi trained as a lawyer in England. He moved to South Africa to work for an Indian law firm. He was shocked by how Indian immigrants were treated there. He devoted his energies to fighting for their rights. He developed a non-violent way to change people's unfair behavior. He called it "devotion to truth." Gandhi was jailed many times, but his work changed how the South African government treated its people.

Around 1915, Gandhi returned to India, which was still largely under British rule. He became an important political figure. His tactic of peaceful non-cooperation eventually changed the way the Indian National Congress operated. He successfully applied pressure to the British by leading thousands of Indians in boycotts of British goods. In 1930, he led a march to protest the British tax on salt. In 1931, clad in sandals and the simple homespun attire of his homeland, Gandhi represented the Indian National Congress at the Round Table Conference in London.

At 53, Gandhi was again thrown in jail. He served two years of a six-year term. When he came out, he decided to devote his energies to improving the relationship between Hindus and Muslims.

In 1945, the British government decided to divide India into two states. India would be for Hindus, and Pakistan would be for Muslims. Gandhi disagreed with this idea. Months of violence followed as the process of splitting the two countries took place. Gandhi wanted to promote peace between the warring religions. He fasted, refusing to eat until it got people's attention. Then he made them promise to be peaceful.

Through his political beliefs, his commitment to non-violence, and his devotion to truth, Gandhi was able to inspire change in those around him and throughout the world.

didn't do very well in his classes. At school, he had a ruler cracked across his knuckles for speaking his native language! Some of the 37 schools he attended with his brother Richard during their youth were segregated by race and ethnicity. Anglos sat with Anglos, Hispanics sat with Hispanics, and Asians with sat with Asians. Everywhere he turned, César felt discriminated against.

César realized that what he was learning at school had nothing to do with the work he and his family did in the farmers' fields. He left school in 1942, at the end of the eighth grade. His father had had an accident, and César didn't want his mother to have to go to work in the fields to support him and his brother.

Many years later, as a grown man and labor leader, César became passionate about education. He kept hundreds of books in his union office and read any time he could. He believed that the purpose of education was to enable him and others to help the oppressed. César Chávez was a true lifelong learner.

The Inspiration Behind the Union

César was inspired by a number of mentors. One of these mentors was a priest named Father Donald McDonnell. César would speak with Father McDonnell at length about strikes and farm workers. He believed in the work of Martin Luther King Jr. and of St. Francis of Assisi. César had also been reading about the famous peace activist, Mohandas Gandhi. All of these men appealed to César's belief in compassion and performing good deeds for the benefit of the poor and weak.

Gandhi had won great political battles in his native India through peaceful, non-violent protest. César agreed with the concept of non-violent protest. He decided it was the route he would take as he fought for migrant farm workers' rights.

Throughout his career as a union organizer, César practiced non-violence in his protest tactics. Sometimes he had to argue against the farm workers themselves when they wanted to turn violent. They believed that no one would listen to their concerns if they practiced non-violence. They wanted to let the world know how angry they felt! César, however, insisted that they could achieve their goals while keeping hold of their dignity.

Fred Ross was another influential person in César's life. He was the first to introduce him to the CSO, the organization that would eventually lead him to join forces with Dolores Huerta to create a union for farm workers. Ross gave César some good ideas. César liked Ross's technique of gathering people together in their homes to talk to them about how working together could help them get what they wanted. Meeting people on their own turf helped them feel comfortable. It helped them trust their union leaders.

After their first house meeting, Ross had good feelings about César. He knew the 25-year-old would one day be capable of accomplishing great things. That night, Ross wrote in his journal: "I think I found the guy I'm looking for."

For years afterward, these important house meetings helped César, Dolores, and their union colleagues expand the union's reach.

Chapter 4
A Union Is Born

In 1962, a frustrated César Chávez resigned from the CSO. Dolores took his advice to keep her job with the CSO for a while before following him. He wanted to make sure his new union strategy would work out successfully. He knew that, with six young children to look after and a seventh on the way, Dolores needed to bring home a regular salary.

Creating the National Farm Workers Association

Dolores remained in Stockton, while César and his family moved to Delano, another town in the San Joaquin Valley. In Delano, César

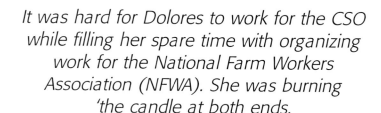

It was hard for Dolores to work for the CSO while filling her spare time with organizing work for the National Farm Workers Association (NFWA). She was burning 'the candle at both ends.

launched the National Farm Workers Association (NFWA). He had help from his wife, Helen, plus a few friends and family members. Even though she was still working at the CSO, Dolores joined as one of the group's leaders. It was an exciting time. "I thought, Wow, we are finally going to do it!" said Dolores many years later. "We are finally going to make it happen."

The pair communicated frequently by mail as César laid plans for how the new organization would be managed. In their letters, they exchanged ideas about their goals for the organization. They talked about strategies for how to reach them.

It was hard for Dolores to work for the CSO while filling her spare time with organizing work for the National Farm Workers Association. She was burning the candle at both ends.

Eventually, in 1964, the CSO fired Dolores. It felt she was giving more of her energies to organizing the emerging NFWA than she was to doing the CSO's own work. She scrambled to make ends meet. She took temporary teaching assignments. She even worked briefly in the fields during the onion harvest. She was not on friendly terms with her former husbands, and they contributed little to support the children.

Dolores continued to work for the NFWA. She spread the word and made people aware of the new organization. She set up meetings and visited workers in their homes and at work camps. She also raised meager dues from the workers, which she and César shared to keep the work moving ahead. She was building a union.

César Chávez and Dolores Huerta are shown at a meeting in 1968. A few years earlier, the two had begun working together to create the organization that would become the United Farm Workers of America (UFW) union.

It was hard for Dolores to drum up money from a group of workers that already had so little. They had a lot to lose, too. They feared their employers might find out. They worried about paying money to the union, because what if they needed that money for when their families fell ill? There were also other union groups that were trying to organize them—and those groups were asking for money.

Many of the farm workers, however, believed strongly in *la causa*, or "the cause," as Dolores called it. They wanted to do what they could to make change happen, so they willingly handed over their fees.

It took a few years for the NFWA to grow. Eventually, Dolores and César got the union to the point where more than 1,000 farm workers were members.

It was hard for Dolores to be a mom and a union organizer at the same time. She grabbed bits and pieces of help wherever she could. She relied on her mother and female relatives to look after her children when she went out to her evening meetings. "So help me, César, without someone to watch my kids," she once wrote, "I just can't find enough time to work, especially in the evenings when it counts."

Despite the hardships she faced, and despite the juggling she had to do to get it all done, Dolores persisted. When she looked back on those broke and stressed-out early years forming the union with César, Dolores recollected, "We really operated totally on faith."

Building a Union, One Person at a Time

One of the main goals of the NFWA was to gather farm workers into labor unions. They wanted to try to hammer out contracts (also known as collective bargaining agreements) with the farmers and commercial growers that the fruit pickers worked for. Dolores was great at inviting people to join the movement. Much of the NFWA's success was a result of Dolores's ability to speak with people and to inspire them to come together and seek change.

The union membership grew slowly at first. In its first year, there were only a handful of members paying their dues. The group worked hard to gradually build up its numbers. NFWA leaders held many house meetings with workers and their families. They reached out to draw in the friends and associates of the workers with whom they spoke. Dolores asked people she knew for advice about how to raise money and set up group insurance plans. She asked for advice on how to get the union's political message across. She learned organizing strategies. She shared this information with César. Together, they figured out how to make it work for the NFWA.

It took a few years for the NFWA to grow. Eventually, Dolores and César got the union to the point where more than 1,000 farm workers were members.

Dolores the Determined

From the start, Dolores was an outspoken champion for farm workers' rights. She passionately communicated the problems of farm workers to the public. Her speeches made people aware of the discrimination and injustice farm workers faced. The 1960s were a time of huge political change in the United States. African-Americans, women, and minorities of all kinds were speaking up. They struggled against economic and political oppression. The National Farm Workers Association struggled right alongside on behalf of migrant farm workers. Dolores's fiery speeches urged people to join the effort to fight against the unfair conditions in the fields. She told people about the way the greedy corporations treated farm workers.

Large-scale growers were so large and so politically powerful that no one had dared to create laws to protect their farm workers.

Dolores's lobbying skills made huge gains for farm workers. She would show up at all hours at pool halls and on front doorsteps, encouraging workers to join the union. She was a tireless,

A Symbol Worthy of Respect

César's brother, Richard, was also active in the NFWA. He designed the eagle symbol that is still used by the union today. César chose the flag's red and black colors. The eagle was a basic Aztec design. It had been simplified so that union members could easily draw it on their own flags of protest. The idea behind the eagle was to show dignity and symbolize the farm workers' pride.

Fasting for Farm Workers

Like Gandhi, César fasted many times. When workers decided to go on strike against major grape growers in 1965, the action triggered a massive campaign that included, in addition to the strike, boycotts and union lobbying. In 1968, César began a fast, going without food and drinking only water for 25 days, in order to raise public awareness of the struggles of the workers. In 1972, he fasted for 24 days. In 1988, he fasted for 36 days. When he finished this final fast, the Reverend Jesse Jackson took it up for three days. Then he passed it along to celebrities and political leaders. Martin Sheen, Emilio Estevez, Danny Glover, and Whoopi Goldberg were among the actors who fasted in support of farm workers, as was Kerry Kennedy, Robert F. Kennedy's daughter.

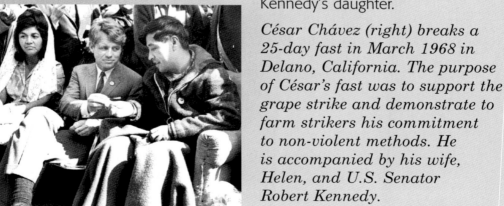

César Chávez (right) breaks a 25-day fast in March 1968 in Delano, California. The purpose of César's fast was to support the grape strike and demonstrate to farm strikers his commitment to non-violent methods. He is accompanied by his wife, Helen, and U.S. Senator Robert Kennedy.

passionate believer. In 1963, Dolores's ability to lobby and negotiate paid off with a big victory. The California State Legislature allowed farm workers access to disability insurance and unemployment insurance programs. It also agreed to allow farm workers to receive money under Aid for Families with Dependent Children, a social welfare program.

They Said It Couldn't Be Done

When Dolores and César announced their plans, their friends said they were crazy. Since World War II, a number of other attempts had been made to organize farm workers. So far, though, the large growers had managed to keep unions from gaining a foothold. The growers had connections with high-ranking political people. Those "friends in high places" had so far helped to prevent union groups from organizing workers.

The farm workers were a huge group of people who worked hard to contribute to American society. Yet they had no voice, and they were powerless to make their own lives better.

There were numerous roadblocks in the way of Dolores and César's success. No laws existed to protect workers. They were paid poorly. They

What Is Lobbying?

Lobbying is a way to persuade lawmakers and government officials to change or create legislation on behalf of a person, a group of people, or an idea. For example, concerned parents might choose to lobby government to change the age limits for issuing drivers' licenses. Or a citizen's group might lobby government to save a historic building, such as an old library.

Lobbying can be done by an individual or a group of individuals. It is always directed toward the people who have the decision-making power. Sometimes governments regulate how, where, and when groups can lobby. Lobbying is a powerful way of influencing how policy (the law) is created.

What Is Collective Bargaining?

Collective bargaining occurs when a group of employees and their employer create a work agreement that is fair to both sides. Bargaining means just that: Workers and the employer bargain back and forth until they've worked out a deal that everyone can agree on. It's a collective agreement because everybody agrees to the terms.

had no legal way to complain or seek better working conditions. Although there were laws in place that allowed some other professions to bargain collectively, there were none for farm workers. Large-scale growers were so large and politically powerful that no one had dared to create laws to protect their farm workers. There was no foundation from which to start.

It was hard to get farmers to agree to deal with unionized workers. No one believed that migrant farm workers could even be organized as a united group. Nearly all of them were poor. Most of them were visible minorities. Many were uneducated. They spoke many different languages, moved around all the time, and most of them didn't have the right to vote. How was it possible to organize such a diverse, constantly changing group of people?

All those reasons, however, were exactly why Dolores and César wanted to form a union to help the farm workers. The farm workers were a huge group of people who worked hard to contribute to American society. Yet they had no voice, and they were powerless to make their own lives better. César and Dolores reasoned that if they could gather together enough of these workers, they would be able to force growers to hear their requests. They felt there was no possible way they could lose.

Dolores and César worked hard. They persevered where others had quit before them. They encouraged people to join the NFWA and rise up against their unfair employers. Together, Dolores Huerta and César Chávez succeeded where others had failed.

They found a way to organize farm workers.

THE 1960s: A HOTBED OF POLITICAL ACTIVISM

Chances are when you think of hippies, you're not thinking about politics, but the two are closely related. In the 1960s, a cultural movement occurred that changed the way people looked at the world. It was a time when people began to question the way things had always been done. Most of the questioning was being done by college-aged kids. These young thinkers began to explore their own beliefs and potential. They created new kinds of music. They started doing things differently than their parents had. Government, and its many layers, frustrated these youngsters. They challenged the existing political structure. Issues such as civil rights and war became subjects of deep discussion.

The decade of the 1960s was, for most Americans, the first time that they and other Americans took a good, hard look at U.S. society on such a large scale. As a result—from issues such as the war in Vietnam to the rights of women and minorities—they began to question many of the values and beliefs they had always thought were important or had taken for granted.

¡VIVA DOLORES!

Chapter 5
Strike Action!

By 1965, Dolores and César had convinced many farm workers and their families from throughout the San Joaquin Valley to come together and work for their common goals. It looked as if their efforts to build a strong union would work after all!

A Call to Battle

Both Dolores and César kept busy schedules. They spoke on behalf of the union and gathered supporters. They were both very popular speakers. Dolores was quick-thinking and easy with language, which made her a natural speaker for the cause. As a Mexican-American woman, she was a unique union leader.

Even so, the union was still young—and not very large. In early September 1965, the

> *Dolores was quick-thinking and easy with language, which made her a natural speaker for the cause. As a Mexican-American woman, she was a unique union leader.*

NFWA leaders were approached by members of the Agricultural Workers Organizing Committee (AWOC). The AWOC was composed mostly of Filipinos. It wanted to launch a strike against some of the largest grape growers in the Delano area of the San Joaquin Valley. Members of AWOC were demanding higher wages. They wanted clean water and access to washrooms. They wanted better treatment from their employers.

On September 16, 1965—timed to coincide with Mexican Independence Day—the National Farm Workers Association (NFWA) voted to strike.

Dolores and César weren't quite ready for such a big labor action. They had wanted to spend a few more years collecting people and getting their group organized before they tried to tackle the big companies in the grape industry. The AWOC members were too angry to wait, however. The strike would have gone ahead anyway, with or without the NFWA. Dolores and César reasoned that they should do all they could to help their Filipino friends. They also understood that by joining the strike they would gain more supporters.

Dolores uses a grape container to transport newspapers, handouts, and other literature on the grape boycott. When Dolores and César Chávez agreed to join another farm workers group in a strike against large grape growers and then organized a boycott of California grapes, they propelled the NFWA to the forefront of the farm workers union movement.

On September 16, 1965—timed to coincide with Mexican Independence Day—the National Farm Workers Association (NFWA) voted to strike. Now that the two groups were combined, they included more than 5,000 farm workers. They walked off the job together, launching the famous Delano Grape Strike.

The following year, the NFWA and the AWOC chose a new name. The group called itself the United Farm Workers Organizing Committee (UFWOC).

Different Strengths, Different Roles

César was an inspiring leader. He was the public face of the farm workers' struggle for their rights. He held marches and engaged in fasts to draw attention to the cause. In contrast, much of Dolores's time was spent behind the scenes. She worked mostly with the union members. She organized people, encouraging them to join the fight for just treatment. She talked to people on the picket lines, keeping their spirits up. She wanted them to use their collective power to show the grape growers that they wouldn't take such poor treatment. She persuaded people into promising that they'd stick together—and stick with the cause. She brought more women into the union and got them involved in fighting for their rights.

When Dolores was on the public stage, she was a powerful speaker. People said she had the gift of persuasion. She was equally comfortable speaking in English or in Spanish. Her words were somehow able to move nearly everyone she talked to. Whether she spoke with farm workers alone or in large rooms packed with students, anti-war activists, or women's groups, her words about the importance of *la causa* (the cause) inspired people to take action.

She was a tough bargainer who stuck to her list of demands. She was unafraid of the businessmen and their lawyers.

Dolores took charge of the union's lobbying efforts. She negotiated on behalf of the farm workers. Dolores was well equipped to hold important discussions with business leaders and politicians. She grew up treating everyone as equals and being treated as an equal. She wasn't afraid of people. She didn't care about how important they were. "I think we really built on each other's strengths a lot," Dolores said about César in a radio interview in 2000:

> *"I think I had more experience in dealing with Anglos than he did ... César was always very uncomfortable because he always felt that politicians would sell you out."*

Dolores was confident and persistent with growers. She never backed down. She was a tough bargainer who stuck to her list of demands. She was unafraid of the businessmen and their lawyers. Dolores put in long hours negotiating with them to get what the farm workers deserved. Sometimes she stayed up all night until a collective agreement was reached, every last detail was covered, every "i" dotted, and every "t" crossed.

Some of the growers called her "The Dragon Lady" because of her fearless negotiating. One Central Valley farmer, with whom Dolores went head to head on several occasions, said, "You don't get anything from Dolores Huerta unless you fight for it and you earn it."

The First Contract:
A Watershed Moment

In 1966, it finally happened. One grape grower, the Schenley Wine Company, sat up and listened to the union's concerns. Dolores was picked to hammer out the first UFWOC contract with the grower. It was the first time in U.S. history that a group of farm workers had reached a collective bargaining agreement with an agricultural company.

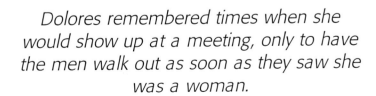

Dolores remembered times when she would show up at a meeting, only to have the men walk out as soon as they saw she was a woman.

In this photo, taken in the 1970s, Dolores is shown standing before a union flag bearing the rallying cry that she helped make famous, "Viva La Causa"—"Long Live the Cause."

¡Viva La Causa!

"*Abajo con opresión!* Down with oppression!" Dolores would shout at the end of her stirring speeches. "*Abajo con racismo!* Down with racism! *Abajo con sexismo!* Down with sexism!"

Her audiences would join her in her rallying cries: "*Viva la union! Viva la causa!* Long live the union! Long live the cause!"

"She went about this stuff with amazing confidence," reflected Harvard instructor and former UFW leader Marshall Ganz. "She went in face to face with these lawyers or professional management people and she was just very impressive. She more than held her own."

Dolores did not consider gender inequality to be one of the causes for which she was fighting. She had, however, become a role model for girls and women.

Dolores stayed on as the UFWOC's tough chief negotiator. She pounded out agreements with businesses that established the first-ever health plans for workers. She also guided more than 100 grievance procedures on behalf of workers. She set up hiring halls. These ensured that employers could only hire unionized workers—not just the cheapest labor they could find. She helped set up farm worker committees at each ranch. Workers could then bring their concerns to the committee members.

Breaking Down Gender Barriers

Dolores was an influential female labor leader in the 1970s. She was nearly the only one holding a top position within a union. "She led

Dolores and César: A Prickly Pair

Dolores and César clashed often. They had very different personalities. Dolores was vocal, aggressive, and unafraid to challenge César's ideas. She had her own ideas to put out there! Most other people did not deal with César Chávez that way.

Dolores had a strong energy and will. She sometimes made life difficult for those closest to her, including César. She wasn't very good at following schedules, she really knew how to hold a grudge and, even though she was a great leader and negotiator, she had trouble keeping things organized.

César was a tolerant boss. He allowed Dolores to act in the way she thought best suited a situation. He helped her focus her thoughts. While César sometimes teased Dolores about her ideas or about her leadership, he admitted that her questions forced him to think carefully about his own ideas. Her prodding helped him make clear decisions.

While César liked that Dolores would speak up and say what she was thinking, the pair certainly had their fights. César fired her many times! Dolores thought nothing of these arguments. Just a couple of days after being fired, she'd be back in the office chatting with César as though nothing had happened. They had a relationship similar to that between siblings.

Dolores felt these arguments with César were healthy. She thought they kept them moving forward. Other people learned to run in the opposite direction when Dolores entered a room César was in!

the picket lines, stared down the bosses, negotiated the contracts, sustained the beatings and carried on," said Karen Nussbaum, past director of the Labor Department's Women's Bureau.

In her line of work, Dolores faced her share of sexism. She was a woman doing what had always been a man's job! Dolores ran into a lot of opposition during the early days of the union. When she was still holding evening meetings with farm workers to convince them to join the NFWA, many of the men she was trying to organize didn't like the fact that she was a woman. They didn't understand a woman who traveled alone long distances and held meetings at night. Dolores remembered times when she would show up at a meeting, only to have the men walk out as soon as they saw she was a woman.

One produce grower grumbled that she was "crazy. She is a violent woman, where women, especially Mexican women, are usually peaceful and calm," he said. Many growers treated Dolores differently than they would have treated a man in her position. The fact that she was a high-profile union leader didn't match their idea of how women should act. They didn't like it.

Despite these challenges to her leadership, Dolores persisted. She was used to breaking down gender barriers in her fight to make farm workers' voices heard. She challenged stereotypes when she heard them pop out of people's mouths. She shot down inappropriate remarks when they were made.

Dolores did not consider gender inequality to be one of the causes for which she was fighting.

LABOR UNIONS: STANDING UP FOR WORKERS' RIGHTS

Labor unions are organizations of workers who have banded together. They share the same goals. Typically, these goals revolve around improving working conditions.

Unions function kind of like governments. Members elect a group of people to act as their leaders. These leaders then bargain with employers on behalf of the union members. Their job is to negotiate the best possible wages, rules, and benefits for their members. It's tough work. Employers rarely want to give more than they absolutely have to.

When a collective agreement is reached and signed by both the employers and the union members, all parties must obey its terms. Workers can't strike unless the union says it's OK. Employers can't change their pay scale without first changing the contract. Unions handle members' complaints (also known as grievances) against their employers. They try to find a fair solution to the problem according to the terms set out in the collective agreement.

Labor unions first rose to popularity in the 1700s and 1800s, during the Industrial Revolution in Europe. Many employers demanded that workers put in long days. Sometimes workers had to do their jobs in dangerous or unhealthy conditions. Back then, workers were often badly treated and underpaid.

She had, however, become a role model for girls and women. At first, she had dismissed the growing women's movement. She called it a "middle-class phenomenon." But she realized that women across America were waking up to the fact that they weren't treated as equals to men. She had been raised by a businesswoman who was active in community politics. Dolores had never really seen women in a passive role. She had always been a feminist, in her actions and in her beliefs.

She began to talk about gender discrimination. She raised issues of sexism in her speeches about the way farm workers were treated. She insisted that the union pay attention to women's issues, such as childcare and sexual harassment. She was troubled that few union leadership roles were held by women—even within her own union. She wanted to see more female leaders.

In the 1970s, Dolores met Gloria Steinem, a well-known feminist thinker. Steinem supported Dolores and the things the union was trying to achieve. Dolores realized she and Gloria Steinem shared similar concerns. Although she did not agree with all of the issues that the feminist movement supported at the time (she did not, for example, support birth control or abortion), she respected the choices of other women.

Dolores added her new understanding of the feminist movement to her campaign. She began to speak to issues concerning women's rights when she pushed leaders for change.

THE FEMINIST MOVEMENT

Feminism—the goal of establishing equal rights and legal protection for women—is not a new idea. The first wave of feminism occurred in the early 1900s. That's when women in the United States and other Western nations began to band together and demand political equality. They wanted the right to vote.

The second wave of feminism came between the 1960s and 1980s. Women fought social and cultural inequalities. They spoke out, demanding that they be treated as men's equals. Feminists demanded that women be paid the same as men for doing the same work. They insisted that women have access to all jobs, including ones traditionally held only by men. They fought for the protection of girls and women from violence and sexual assault. They fought for women to have access to birth control, abortions, and shelters to keep them safe from abusive partners. They demanded that men treat women with respect. Women were tired of being treated simply as objects or anything less than a full-fledged person.

The second wave of feminism was led mostly by white, middle-class women. It didn't exactly represent everyone's views equally. Many feminists said the problem of racism had to be addressed first, before trying to address issues of gender inequality. That way, feminists of all different ethnic backgrounds could work together to strengthen women's position in society.

In the 1990s, a third wave of feminism began. It includes women from all racial backgrounds—not just whites. Third-wave feminist thinkers don't always agree with earlier feminists. They are open to different opinions of what feminism means, and they often debate feminist issues— such as fundamental differences between men and women— that earlier feminists may have felt would encourage sexual discrimination.

Chapter 6
Fighting the Good Fight

Dolores's work was important. She was a passionate speaker. She called the public's awareness to issues that nobody else was talking about. She used her speaking abilities to educate people about the union's goals. She generated support for the labor movement. It was an uphill battle much of the time.

When Work Makes You Sick

Dolores spoke to as many people as she could about toxic pesticides. She wanted people to know that these poisons sickened workers, the environment, and the people who ate the fruit that the farm workers picked. When migrant farm workers kept showing up with the same

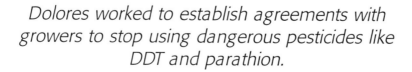

Dolores worked to establish agreements with growers to stop using dangerous pesticides like DDT and parathion.

health problems over and over, the UFWOC kept careful track. It found a variety of cancers in many of the farm workers living in the San Joaquin Valley. Dolores worked to establish agreements with growers to stop using dangerous pesticides like DDT and parathion.

Leading the Way for Change

Dolores was one of UFWOC's most visible spokespersons. In the late 1960s, she lobbied the governments in Sacramento and in Washington, D.C., for changes to farm workers' conditions. She organized field strikes. She directed UFWOC boycotts. Dolores knew how important it was to drum up high-level support for her cause. She made connections with political and religious groups that could help the UFWOC. She led farm workers in supporting the campaigns of progressive or liberal-leaning Democratic political candidates such as Senator Robert F. Kennedy and others who came after him.

In the face of the grape growers' continued injustices, the strike took on greater importance. The union wanted the public to see the strike not just as an issue about wages. It wanted people to see it as a social justice issue.

A picture that speaks volumes about the need for changes in the conditions under which farm workers used to labor. This young girl is pouring onions that she has collected into a burlap sack for packaging, near Mettler, California, in 1976. The girl worked the onion fields in her socks so she could save her shoes for school and special days. She was paid 35 cents for every 40 pounds (18 kg) of onions that she collected in a discarded pesticide container.

Speaking Out about Grape Growers

The Delano Grape Strike that began in 1965 carried on for five years. As the strike dragged on, California grape growers began to worry about losing money. Some of the growers offered to raise wages and provide health care to their workers. Most of them, however, refused to meet any of the grape pickers' demands. Instead, growers looked for help from the state and federal governments. They didn't want to give in to farm workers. They thought it would cost too much money. The growers also had help from workers from across the border who were quite willing to pick grapes for less than the UFWOC's wage.

In the face of the grape growers' continued injustices, the strike took on greater importance. The union wanted the public to see the strike not just as an issue about wages. It wanted people to see it as a social justice issue. Dolores and the UFWOC reached out to an even wider audience. They drew student activists, church groups, and even some other unions, such as the United Auto Workers, into their circle of support.

Dolores helped make consumers aware of the grape strike. She encouraged them to boycott grapes. That would send an even stronger message to growers. She headed to the East Coast of the United States, where most grapes and wine were sold. She spoke to women's organizations, church groups, and student groups, and on radio talk shows. She had brought along a busload of farm workers and student volunteers. These people collected donations and recruited people to pick up signs

PRAISE FROM ON HIGH

At a formal speech on June 4, 1968, Dolores Huerta stood next to Robert F. Kennedy onstage. He was running for president. Kennedy praised Dolores for helping him win the 1968 California Democratic Presidential Primary. She had thrown her support behind him, and the union members had followed. The union's support gave him a big boost from Mexican-American voters.

    Moments after he thanked Dolores and the farm workers, Kennedy was tragically shot and killed as he walked through the kitchen of the Ambassador Hotel in Los Angeles. The man who shot him was 24 at the time. He remains in a California state prison to this day.

that said "Boycott California Grapes!" From there, the effort spread to other eastern cities.

Boycott California Grapes!

The public was shocked. They had no idea how unfairly farm workers were being treated. Consumers jumped on board and joined the boycott. Grapes rotted in grocery stores across the country. People simply refused to buy them. Dolores's boycott stirred many people to show their support for the farm workers' cause. Peace groups, other unions, student protesters, community organizations, political activists, Hispanic associations, religious groups, and concerned consumers—all of them stood behind the farm workers. The grape boycotts saw more than 14 million Americans throw their weight behind the cause. Dolores's leadership during the grape boycotts was so strong that she inspired other groups to reach for their goals, too.

The boycott was very successful. The entire California table grape industry eventually gave in to workers' demands. In 1970, the Delano

"Dolores had a gift for making you believe in yourself ... She has an ability to inspire you and urge you to do things you could not think were possible. She is one of those life-changers."

Eliseo Medina, a former UFW vice-president. Medina himself was once a young grape picker.

This photo was taken in 1976 at a Pittsburgh rally in support of the United Farm Workers (UFW) grape boycott.

Consumers jumped on board and joined the boycott. Grapes rotted in grocery stores across the country. People simply refused to buy them.

and Coachella grape growers finally agreed to sign a collective bargaining agreement with the UFWOC. Workers would be protected from dangerous pesticides. They would get fresh water and public toilets in the fields. They would have access to a medical plan. The growers agreed to provide these things for at least the length of a three-year contract.

The strike had lasted five years. At long last, grape pickers were given the same rights and benefits that other American workers had enjoyed for years.

The Ugly Side of Doing Battle

The grape strikes had shown growers that the UFWOC was a strong enemy. Other commercial growers decided they didn't want any part of this fierce union. The moment the Delano Grape Strike was settled by UFWOC contracts, California lettuce growers turned around and signed a deal with the Teamsters Union. They figured if the unions were headed their way, they might as well sign with one that wasn't as tough as the UFWOC. The Teamsters had a reputation for being a corrupt organization. Their contracts—commonly referred to as containing "sweetheart deals" for growers— didn't protect workers at all. This suited lettuce growers just fine. They didn't care about the workers. They only cared about keeping the UFWOC out.

The Teamsters contracts gave lettuce workers no wage increases. They did nothing to protect workers from pesticides. When workers found out about the sweetheart deals, they were furious. They walked out on strike.

THE DOWNSIDE OF PESTICIDES

Pesticides have been used for centuries by humans to prevent insects and diseases from harming crops. As far back as ancient Mesopotamia (the region that includes modern-day Iraq), growers sprinkled sulfur around their gardens. Pesticides are used today in many large farming businesses. They are sprayed onto crops by tractors, airplanes, or people carrying spray packs on their backs.

While they have their advantages, pesticides have been linked to health problems in animals and humans. Until the mid-1970s, DDT was used in the United States as a very effective bug killer. People sprayed it on their crops—and on their bodies. Studies showed, however, that DDT prevented some birds from reproducing. It also caused human babies to be born too early. DDT is still used in developing countries to control malaria (a disease spread by mosquitoes).

Parathion causes seizures, vision problems, and swelling of the lungs and can even stop you from breathing. Workers exposed to parathion over a long period of time may suffer memory and skin problems. They can get cancer and depression, and their unborn babies may develop birth conditions leading to problems with brain functioning.

Pesticides can travel on air currents or in water from farmers' fields into drainage ditches. From there, they spread into rivers and oceans. Sometimes they kill species other than the ones they are intended to control. Pesticides show up at all levels of the food chain. They have been found in deadly concentrations in advanced predators like eagles or wolves. Some 2.5 million tons of pesticides are used around the world every year. The World Health Organization estimates that about 18,000 farm workers die each year from pesticide poisoning.

In 1973, the grape contracts expired. The UFWOC was now the United Farm Workers of America (UFW), and grape growers didn't want to be bound by another strict UFW contract. They copied what the lettuce growers had done. They opted to sign sweetheart deals with the Teamsters union instead.

Bad feelings between the unions sprang up. Teamsters were hired to threaten and attack UFW farm workers who were striking in Los Angeles. In 1974, two UFW workers were killed on the picket lines. Many people were thrown in jail. Dolores and César begged their supporters not to fight. They encouraged them to follow the UFW's commitment to non-violence.

Dolores spoke out publicly. She spurred consumers into action. She told them not to buy food from the corporations responsible for the workers' deaths. More strikes and another public grape boycott followed. This time, the boycott expanded to include lettuce and Gallo wines. Dolores and the UFW continued to help grape pickers. They began to organize vegetable workers, too.

Victory in the Form of the Law

Dolores had managed to pull off some pretty powerful boycotts that had involved consumers across the whole country. Partly because of this, the California state legislature passed the 1975 Agricultural Labor Relations Act. The law gave California farm workers the right to organize into unions. It allowed them to bargain for better working conditions and wages. It set out guidelines for how labor disagreements in the fields would be handled. The Act also let workers

In 1972, the UFWOC became the United Farm Workers of America (UFW). At its peak during the 1970s, the union had about 100,000 dues-paying members. Dolores Huerta (far right) poses for a group portrait with the Board of Directors of the United Farm Workers of America (UFW). Standing, left to right: Marshall Ganz, Phillip Vera Cruz, Richard Chávez, Pete Velasco. Sitting, left to right: Mack Lyons, César Chávez, Gilbert Padilla, Eliseo Medina, and Dolores Huerta.

Dolores did not agree with the idea that women belonged only at home. She didn't want to spend her life cooking and cleaning and making life easy for the man and children of the house.

choose their union by electing them. It was the first farm labor law of its kind in the country.

After the Agricultural Labor Relations Act passed, farm workers voted to have the UFW represent them as their union. They didn't want the Teamsters representing them. The lettuce contracts had shown workers that the Teamsters weren't fair. The Teamsters were edged out by the UFW.

Around the time of the national boycotts, Dolores began a romantic relationship with Richard Chávez, César's brother. Over the years, Dolores had four children with Richard: Juanita, María Elena, Ricky, and Camilla. At the time, women with families were expected to devote most of their energy to their children. People criticized her for putting so much effort into her work at the expense of her 11 children, as well as for living with Richard to whom she was not married. Her family and union colleagues disagreed with her. Even her friends thought she was doing things all wrong. Dolores loved her kids, and she loved her job.

"I think had it not been for the women's movement, I never would have had the courage to do what I did to get involved with him."

The Busiest Mom Ever?

Dolores was married twice and had children by three different men. She was not your average Mexican-American woman! But then again, neither was her own mother. Dolores did not agree with the idea that women belonged only at home. She didn't want to spend her life making life easy for the man and children of

A Feminist,
a Leader,
a Mexican–American

Dolores was a true trailblazer because she was all three. She proudly identified herself as a Chicana (a woman of Mexican heritage). She could trace the roots of her social activism to the time when she first felt the sting of anti-Mexican discrimination back in her school days. Joining the Stockton Community Service Organization (CSO) was her first step in joining the fight for civil rights. She understood the struggles of Mexican farm workers who were shoved to the fringes of society. That was partly why she joined with César Chávez to form the National Farm Workers union. Dolores understood what it was like for the lower class to struggle against the unfair practices of their wealthy bosses. She had seen it all her life.

Dolores was particularly aware of the issues faced by minority women. They faced racism, gender discrimination, and unfair treatment by their employers. It was a triple whammy.

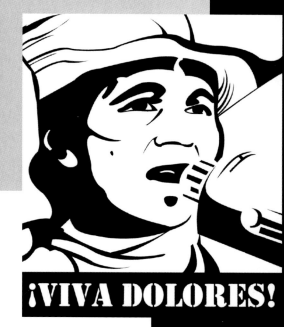

¡VIVA DOLORES!

the house. That's not to say she didn't like being a mother. She did. She loved children, and she adored her own kids. She insisted that having children fulfilled a special need for her.

One time, she even said that God must have seen her as lucky by having blessed her with so many children. Dolores felt that raising children wasn't her only duty, however. She thought if a woman wanted to be part of life outside the home, then she should enjoy that opportunity.

Dolores admits that each of her 11 daughters and sons had to make sacrifices for her career. César had his wife, Helen, to look after their eight children. Dolores had no such partner. She was both the mother and the worker. Her children knew from very early on that their mother's truest passion was to help farm workers in need. She was away from home a lot. She forgot to pick her kids up from school sometimes. Sometimes they had to eat supper at friends' houses or crash with relatives when she wasn't home. Dolores took her kids along with her to work sometimes, when she couldn't arrange for childcare. She missed birthdays and school functions. Once the family even drove to school on a tire that had been slashed by somebody who was upset

"Before I joined the union, I was having a hard time really swallowing that I would be a teacher living in a suburb ... My longings for my own life were answered by being able to participate in the building of the union."

Dolores Huerta

Non-Violence Is Our Strength

Dolores wanted whole families to join the union because often children worked in the fields, too. She insisted that union activities be free from violence to keep everyone safe. Dolores considered every life to be precious. She reasoned that if workers were struggling for their dignity, it wouldn't make any sense for them to do it in a violent manner.

Over her career as a lobbyist and political activist, Dolores was arrested a total of 22 times. Each time, it was for participating in non-violent peaceful union activities.

Honored to Be Poor

Dolores was not the kind of person who wanted the "finer things in life." She had turned away from a teaching career, which would have made a lot more money.

For many years, Dolores refused to accept a full salary from the UFW. She elected to receive only $5 a week. Many other union members did the same. Dolores made many sacrifices for her work. She relied on donations and the goodwill of friends and family to help meet her own family's needs.

> *"I guess the political and the work has always come first with me and then I just tried to catch up on the other because I often felt that for every unmade bed and for every unwashed dish some farm worker got one more dollar in wages somewhere. You know, some family out there was made better. And it's sort of the decision that I made and thank God my children, you know, understood that decision."*
>
> Dolores Huerta in a radio interview, 2000

with her union work.

Sometimes, Dolores's children were jealous and resentful of the farm workers. They knew in their hearts, however, that she was doing important work.

Always One More Person

Dolores loved her work. She traveled from meetings to rallies to speaking dates. Even though it was exhausting, she also found it energizing. She loved the feeling that came from getting people together and focusing their energies on a single cause. "You could just feel this power you could generate from people working together," she said. "It was just very awesome. We were doing what we loved and so we didn't really sacrifice anything."

She was living her beliefs. She set an example for her children of how to be a responsible and involved person in the world.

Nearly all of Dolores's children have worked in some way for the union. Today, one is a doctor. One is a nurse. One is a lawyer. One is a public health specialist. One is a chef, and almost all of them work to make life better for others. It's a fact that makes Dolores's heart sing.

Richard Chávez and Dolores Huerta, two of the leading activists for the United Farm Workers of America (UFW), pose for a portrait in La Paz, California, in 1994. Richard and Dolores have had four children together.

"We understood very quickly she wasn't ours to have ... She sort of belonged to the farm worker movement. And it was our job to support her."

Dolores's son Emilio, who is now a lawyer for the National Farm Workers Service Center

Chapter 7
Meeting Challenges Head On

The UFW won hundreds of elections between 1975 and 1980. Many groups of farm workers wanted the UFW to represent them. They knew the UFW worked hard to make sure workers got what they needed.

The Growers Strike Back

Not all of the elections led to the union signing contracts with growers, however. Growers found plenty of ways to slow down negotiations. They tried every tactic to stall. They used legal loopholes to slow deals down. To make things

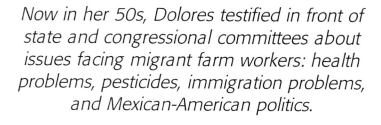

Now in her 50s, Dolores testified in front of state and congressional committees about issues facing migrant farm workers: health problems, pesticides, immigration problems, and Mexican-American politics.

worse, boycotts had been declared illegal by this time. The UFW couldn't even appeal to the public for support, as it had during the grape boycotts.

California farmers found many ways to avoid paying fair wages to the unionized workers who picked the fruits and vegetables in their fields. They refused to cooperate with the UFW and continued to illegally hire undocumented immigrants as in years past. These people were willing to work longer hours for less pay. The majority of farmers were more than happy to hire these non-unionized workers.

Internal Conflict Weakens the Union

In the late 1970s, Dolores became the director of the UFW's Citizenship Participation Day Department. This was the political arm of the union. Her job was to lobby the California state legislature to protect the new farm labor law.

Around this time, the UFW began losing ground. There were fewer elections. Union leaders fought a lot. César believed that bad people within the union were trying to overthrow him. The movement weakened. Not as many people wanted to join up. Organizing drives weakened. Some union members began asking for more pay, which the bosses didn't like. People inside the union couldn't agree whether the UFW should continue to try to organize people in the fields. Everyone was arguing.

In 1981, a group of dissatisfied union members rebelled and tried to elect their own candidates to the UFW board. The union leaders were angry. Dolores was sent to Salinas to control the uprising. She fired ten of the

This mural depicts the struggle for basic human rights, some of them children and mothers holding babies. The woman at the lower right appears to be in a state of despair, in contrast to the look of determination on the face of the woman at the upper right. Along with the broken chain and the raised fists, this woman suggests the hope that lies behind the united efforts of the people.

rebels outright. She said they were not working hard enough on behalf of migrant farm workers, but critics said César had grown a bit too hungry for power. They said the union would only accept new members who promised to be faithful to César. The union, they said, would only tolerate members who supported all of its actions.

Throughout the 1980s, many of the people who had helped start the union left or were fired. Of all the original leaders, only Dolores and César remained.

The slow slide of the once powerful United Farm Workers had begun.

Reaching Out to a Wider Audience

In 1982, with the huge support—and financial backing—of big farming interests, Republican George Deukmejian was elected governor of California. With such a powerful anti-union governor now in office, and his political appointees basically refusing to enforce the 1975 Agricultural Labor Relations Act, the union's strength was further weakened.

The UFW's numbers shrank through the 1980s. The union decided to turn its focus outward. It reached out to the U.S. public to talk about the dangers of pesticides. Dolores continued her role as a communicator for the union and helped found the UFW's own radio station. She also continued her speaking and fundraising work. Now in her 50s, Dolores testified in front of state and congressional committees about issues facing migrant farm workers: health problems, pesticides, immigration problems, and Mexican-American politics.

She lobbied the federal government to grant amnesty to farm workers who had lived, worked, and paid taxes in the United States for many years and yet were not given the same rights as U.S. citizens. Dolores's work in this regard helped bring about the Immigration Reform and Control Act of 1986. The Act made it against the law for employers to hire people who were not legally allowed to work in the country. It granted amnesty to certain undocumented immigrants who had arrived in the United States before 1982. The Act also sped up the immigration process for farm workers who were working illegally in the United States.

Dolores still fights for amnesty for undocumented immigrants to this day.

In 1988, Dolores was badly injured during a peaceful protest in San Francisco …
She was knocked to the ground and clubbed with police batons.

Life in a Slower Lane

In 1988, Dolores was badly injured during a peaceful protest in San Francisco. People had gathered to protest the policies of presidential candidate George H. W. Bush. Outside a hotel

where Mr. Bush was speaking, Dolores was handing out news releases about the UFW. She was knocked to the ground and clubbed with police batons. The attack was captured on camera. Several of Dolores's ribs were broken. Her spleen was badly damaged. She was rushed to a hospital for emergency surgery to remove her spleen. Her doctors feared she might not live. She was 58.

Dolores sued the city of San Francisco for her injuries. She eventually received a record out-of-court settlement of $825,000. As a result of the incident, the San Francisco Police Department changed its crowd-control policies.

It took Dolores many months to recover after the San Francisco incident. She took some time off from her union work and focused on women's rights instead. She toured the country speaking on behalf of women, encouraging Latinas to run for office. Dolores participated in the Feminist Majority's Feminization of Power: 50/50 by 2000 campaign. She wanted to see more Hispanic women in political roles.

Dolores was pleased by the role she played in boosting ethnic women's representation in office. As a result of the campaign, there was a large increase in the number of women representatives at the local, state, and federal levels of government.

For a number of years following her recovery, Dolores continued her work for the union. She traveled the country promoting *la causa* and women's rights. Together with César Chávez, Dolores helped get many health, benefit, and pension plans for farm workers. César described his long-time colleague as "totally fearless, both mentally and physically."

Even with these successes, the 1990s were a tough time for the farm workers' movement. Internal union politics left people feeling uneasy. The political climate had shifted from where it had been in the 1960s and 1970s, when the labor movement was strong. Now the feeling was more conservative. People didn't feel that the needs of migrant farm workers were as pressing as they once had been. They had forgotten about the farm workers' problems. The UFW continued to lose ground.

Then, in 1993, the union was dealt a heavy blow.

Death of a Leader

At the age of 66, César Chávez died. No one saw it coming, and it threw the union into a crisis. Many wondered whether the UFW could even continue without its leader.

¡VIVA DOLORES!

César had been in San Luis, Arizona, helping UFW lawyers defend the union. The UFW was being sued by a giant California vegetable producer. The company wanted the union to pay it back the millions of dollars that it had lost during the boycotts of previous years. After a day supporting the farm workers in court, César ate supper. He went up to his hotel room, where he stayed up late reading.

It was a habit of his.

When César still had not left his room by 9 a.m. the next morning, his colleagues entered. Lying on the bed, still fully clothed, was César Chávez. He had died peacefully in his sleep.

In his right hand was a book on Native American crafts. On his face was a smile.

President Obama Declares César Chávez Day

On the date of what would have been César Chávez's 83rd birthday, U.S. President Barack Obama announced a national day of celebration. On March 31, 2010, the president held a special meeting to announce the news. He invited Dolores Huerta, current UFW president Arturo Rodriguez, and several of César's family members.

"Obama told us that without the example of César Chávez perhaps he would not have become president," said Dolores. "The president reminded us that he began his career as a community organizer and followed César's example." In fact, Mr. Obama's 2008 election campaign used a version of the UFW slogan, *"Si, se puede!"* ("Yes, we can!")

By proclaiming César Chávez Day, Mr. Obama hopes Americans will make an effort to serve their communities to honor the legacy of César Chávez.

"ONCE SOCIAL CHANGE BEGINS, IT CANNOT BE REVERSED.

YOU CANNOT UNEDUCATE THE PERSON WHO HAS LEARNED TO READ.

YOU CANNOT HUMILIATE THE PERSON WHO FEELS PRIDE.

YOU CANNOT OPPRESS THE PEOPLE WHO ARE NOT AFRAID ANYMORE."

—CESAR CHAVEZ
MARCH 31, 1927–APRIL 23, 1993

CESAR CHAVEZ DAY MARCH 31, 2010
DÍA DE CÉSAR CHÁVEZ EL 31 DE MARZO 2010

U.S. Department of Labor
Hilda L. Solis, Secretary of Labor

A downloadable version is available on LaborNet.

Chapter 8
Still Fighting for the Underdog

Even with César gone, Dolores didn't quit. Now that the union was without a leader, she found it even more important to keep up the fight. She renewed her activist efforts. With her constant power cry of *"Si, se puede!"* she kept on working.

The Show Must Go On

When César Chávez died in 1993, his son-in-law, Arturo Rodriguez, took over the presidency of the United Farm Workers. Arturo Rodriguez had a renewed interest in taking the union back to its roots in the fields. He wanted to organize strawberry, wine, grape, and mushroom workers.

In a stretch of 40 years, Dolores took one vacation ... Otherwise, it's been business as usual for this busy organizer.

Dolores Huerta has never felt like giving up on fighting for farm workers' rights. As she said in 1999:

"There is just so much work to be done, and someone has to do it. In organizing, you are not going to reach every person, but you just have to keep pushing for the next one."

In a stretch of 40 years, Dolores took one vacation—a week in Puerto Vallarta, Mexico, with her son. Otherwise, it's been business as usual for this busy organizer.

Dolores worked as the union's secretary-treasurer until 1999. She stepped down then and took the title of vice-president emeritus. She spent her time advocating for women. She also worked on the presidential campaign of Al Gore. By this time, union membership had dipped to 25,000, and only 10 percent of migrant farm workers in the United States belonged to the UFW. The starting union wage was $10.45 an hour—but nearly 75 percent of farm workers made less than half that.

In 2000, Dolores fell sick with an abdominal illness. She was forced to stay in the hospital for a long period. It took her a while to recover—but her fighting spirit got her through. Recover she did, and she went straight back to work.

The Dolores Huerta Foundation Is Born

Now in her 80s, Dolores Huerta has 20 grandchildren and five great-grandchildren. She continues to work with people who are

Dolores Huerta (in black jacket) marches in the front row of a United Farm Workers union rally in Los Angeles in 2006. Now in her 80s, Dolores continues to work as a leader in the fight to bring equality, fair pay, and social justice to those without a voice of their own.

unfairly treated. As president of the Dolores Huerta Foundation, she advocates for women, children, and the working poor. She works to develop leaders who will take on the role of advocating for those who don't have a voice. Dolores's work takes her to universities and meetings where she speaks with people about issues of social justice.

Even today in the San Joaquin Valley, thousands of working poor immigrants don't have a voice. They don't speak the language or understand the laws. They don't have any personal power, and they don't know which agencies can protect them. They feel helpless, and they are at risk of being taken advantage of. As always, Dolores seeks to show these individuals that they do indeed have the power to change and improve their lives—especially if they work together.

Dolores arranges meetings to empower these poor immigrant workers. In these organizational meetings, small groups of farm workers come together in people's homes. A trained organizer shows how they can achieve powerful changes by working together toward a common goal. Then, after a total of 200 people have attended the house meetings, they are brought together to form a large group. They elect a committee to oversee the group. The group then joins the *Vecinos Unidos*—the United Neighbors. The group holds monthly meetings about issues such as immigration, health, and safety.

"The main purpose of organizing is to develop leadership," Dolores once said. "And to develop leadership ... the people you are organizing have to own the organization, and

¡Sí, Se Puede!

Even today, the United Farm Workers still use the organizing cry of "*Sí, se puede!*" Literally translated, it means, "Yes, it can be done!" César and Dolores developed the motto during one of César's fasts. It's a rallying call that inspires people to support the cause. It reminds people of the union's commitment to a "personal and organizational spirit that promotes confidence, courage and risk taking."

"I think we brought to the world, the United States anyway, the whole idea of boycotting as a non-violent tactic. I think we showed the world that non-violence can work to make social change ... I think we have laid a pattern of how farm workers are eventually going to get out of their bondage. It may not happen right now in our foreseeable future, but the pattern is there and farm workers are going to make it."

Dolores Huerta

The Dolores Huerta Foundation

Dolores Huerta and César Chávez dedicated their lives to seeking justice for the working poor. The Dolores Huerta Foundation ensures that this fight will continue in the future. The goal of the foundation is to inspire a new generation of community leaders. These people will continue the work that César and Dolores started. They will visit people in their communities and work to organize them so that they may pursue social justice.

for them to own the organization, they've got to take it over." Dolores and César wanted not just for the people at the top to always be barking orders. They wanted the workers to be the ones to take charge and make the decisions. "So, this is why when we started the union, César and myself, you know, we wanted to try and make it a little different."

Dolores's work continues to this day. Bit by bit, she hopes to continue to show mistreated people that they can combine their voices and be heard.

Leaving Behind a Legacy

Dolores's work with the UFW has left a legacy for the Hispanic community in the United States. She has especially touched the lives of the working poor who were living on the fringes of American society.

Her voice—constant, pressing, and certain—draws the nation's attention to the problems of the migrant farm workers whose hands help put food on tables across the country.

Dolores Huerta's legacy expands across a territory even wider than the UFW. Yes, she has worked as a civil rights advocate, fighting for migrant farm workers' rights, but she has also been a champion of feminism, peace, and the environment. She has voiced her concerns about human rights.

She spoke out early against pesticide use. It's an issue our society has only just begun to talk

"[Dolores Huerta] is the hardest working, most determined yet optimistic crusader for people I have ever met. She thinks nothing of taking a red-eye flight from California to New York or elsewhere and then a red-eye on to somewhere else. She is tireless."

Eleanor Smeal, president of the advocacy group The Feminist Majority Foundation

It's Not All Just About César!

For years, the world talked only about César Chávez and the success he achieved through his work with the UFW. Historians and journalists and even politicians only acknowledged César's contributions to the labor movement. Many articles and books have been written about César Chávez. There was far less attention paid to his partner and union co-founder. Until recently, no one really stopped to consider that César didn't do it all himself. He had a lot of help from a strong-voiced and smart woman named Dolores Huerta.

¡VIVA CESAR!

Dolores Huerta wrote..." Cesar's life is the lucero, the light that provides vision to our path, with the glow of energy generated by the struggle"

Cesar Chavez once described Huerta's character as "totally fearless, both mentally and physically."

¡VIVA DOLORES!

about. "While few, if any, can fill her shoes," said Paul Chávez, son of the late César Chávez, "many will follow in her footsteps."

Dolores Huerta was a young woman who fully understood her equality to the men around her. She has served as a role model for generations of women of Mexican heritage. Throughout her life, she has given voice to the concerns of thousands who had no voice of their own. "It was Dolores who showed us not to be afraid to fight for a better life for ourselves and our children," said one farm worker during a tribute to Dolores. "And she did it at a time when women didn't have a voice."

OUTSTANDING ACCOMPLISHMENTS

Dolores Huerta has received numerous awards for her tireless work on behalf of others. In 1984, the California State Senate honored Dolores with the Outstanding Labor Leader Award. In 1993, she was inducted into the National Women's Hall of Fame. That same year, the American Civil Liberties Union presented her with the Roger Baldwin Medal of Liberty Award. She has received the Eleanor Roosevelt Human Rights Award, bestowed by President Bill Clinton in 1998, as well as many other awards and distinctions. Dolores has received nine honorary doctorates from universities throughout the United States, and many schools have been named in her honor.

Chronology

1848 Migrant farm workers begin entering the United States from Mexico.

1869 Mohandas Gandhi is born. Gandhi would serve as one of César Chávez's most influential role models.

1927 César Chávez is born March 31.

1930 Dolores Fernandez is born April 10 in a New Mexico mining town.

mid-1930s Dolores's parents divorce. Dolores and her brothers and mother move away and eventually settle in Stockton, California.

1942 The Bracero Program begins. Mexican workers are brought into the United States to help in the fields. They work willingly for little money. César Chávez quits school to work in the fields and help his family survive.

1948 Fred Ross founds the Community Service Organization (CSO) with the help of several Mexican-Americans.

1950 Dolores marries Ralph Head. They have two daughters.

1950s Farm workers have no access to social security benefits or health insurance. Life expectancy is 49 years.

1953 Dolores divorces Ralph Head.

1955 Dolores helps Fred Ross establish the Stockton CSO chapter.

late 1950s Dolores marries Ventura Huerta. They have five children.

1958 Dolores and several other CSO supporters found the Agricultural Workers Association (AWA) under the CSO banner.

1961 César Chávez decides he must start a union to protect migrant farm workers.

1963 Dolores secures disability insurance and other benefits for farm workers.

1964 Religious, ethnic, and labor groups succeed in ending the Bracero Program. The Stockton CSO fires Dolores.

1965 California grape pickers make about 90 cents per hour, plus two cents per full basket picked. An estimated 466,000 migrant farm workers are working in U.S. fields. This group comprises people of many ethnic backgrounds.

1965–1970 The Delano Grape Strike. It ends by growers signing three-year contracts with the UFWOC.

1968 Presidential candidate Robert F. Kennedy is shot and killed on June 4, moments after publicly thanking Dolores Huerta for her support.

late 1960s Dolores launches the first national boycott of grapes. She meets Richard Chávez. Over the years, they have four children together.

1972 The UFWOC changes its name to the United Farm Workers of America (UFW).

1973 The original UFWOC grape contracts expire. Instead of re-signing with UFW, growers sign sweetheart deals with the Teamsters union.

1975 The California state legislature passes the Agricultural Labor Relations Act, giving California farm workers the right to organize into unions and bargain for better working conditions and wages.

1981 An angry UFW group tries to elect its own candidates to the union board. The union has started its slow slide away from power.

1982 George Deukmejian, a Republican with financial backing from big farming interests, is elected governor of California. With a powerful anti-union governor in office and his appointees refusing to enforce the 1975 Agricultural Labor Relations Act, the union's strength is further weakened.

1986 The U.S. government passes the Immigration Reform and Control Act. It grants amnesty to many illegal Mexican immigrants.

1988 At age 58, Dolores is beaten by police during a peaceful protest in San Francisco. She nearly dies.

1993 César Chávez dies. César's son-in-law, Arturo Rodriguez, takes over presidency of the United Farm Workers. Dolores continues working as Union's Secretary-Treasurer.

1999 Dolores retires as the UFW's secretary-treasurer. She spends her time advocating for women, children, and the working poor, and building the Dolores Huerta Foundation.

2010 Still an activist, Dolores delivers speeches about social injustice at meetings and universities.

Glossary

activism The action of bringing about social, political, economic, or environmental change by trying to persuade others to change their behavior

agricultural Related to the production of food and goods through farming

amnesty An act where a government accepts and pardons people who may have been guilty of an offense against it

Anglo English speaking

boycott Protesting by refusing to purchase an item or support a company

braceros Mexican workers who were brought into the United States under an agreement between the U.S. and Mexican governments beginning in 1942 until 1964, allowing them to work for very low wages in U.S. fields

civil rights The rights of a nation's citizens to social and political freedom and equality

commercial Having to do with the production of a commodity, such as a crop, for sale

displaced Forced out of an area

diversity Having many different cultures, ethnic backgrounds, and races

drought A period of prolonged dryness due to lack of rain or snowfall

exploitation Being unfairly used or taken advantage of

grievance A wrong suffered by a worker that serves as grounds for a complaint

honorary doctorate A degree granted by a university that is not based on a course of study, but is given to recognize a person's contribution to society

Industrial Revolution A time in the 1700s and 1800s when major advances in farming and other industries in Europe and North America led to more work being done by machines, increases in productivity, and changes in nations' cultures and economies

insurance A system in which, in exchange for money paid regularly into a general fund, a company, government, or other organization guarantees compensation in the event of certain kinds of losses, injuries, or death

labor Related to work and workers

lobby To seek to influence the passage of certain types of laws

loophole A weakness or ambiguity in a law or set of rules that allows people to get around having to obey the law

mentor A trusted friend, counselor, or teacher who advises and provides an example for a less experienced person

migrant Traveling from place to place, with no fixed address

negotiate To discuss a topic with the goal of reaching an agreement between two sides

oppressed Mistreated by another group; not allowed full expression and freedom

pension A wage paid to a worker after he or she has retired, usually based on the worker's regular payments into a fund

pesticide A substance applied to a crop to reduce the chances that pests will harm the crop

picket lines Boundaries set by workers on strike that others are asked not to cross

poverty level A "line" below which not enough money exists to provide the basic necessities of life, such as adequate food, shelter, and clothing

sediments Fine layers of rock, sand, and soil that settle at the bottom of a lake

segregation Separating according to race, class, or ethnicity

sexism The unfair treatment of a person based on his or her sex

social worker A person who works for a government or other social agency to try to help people meet their needs and improve their quality of life

toxic Poisonous

transition The process of moving from place to place; a change

unconventional Unusual; different than what is usually done

undocumented Lacking official immigration papers

union A coalition of workers who elect people to represent them in dealing with employers

war bonds Documents that people can purchase from the government in a time of war that help fund the war effort. If the nation wins the war, the bonds may be cashed in for a modest return in addition to the original amount invested.

Further Information

Books

Doak, Robin S. *Dolores Huerta: Labor Leader and Civil Rights Activist.*
North Mankato, MN: Compass Point, 2008.

de Ruiz, Dana Catharine, and Richard Larios. *La Causa: The Migrant Farmworkers' Story.* Raintree Steck-Vaughn, 1992.

Ferriss, Susan, and Ricardo Sandoval. *The Fight in the Fields: Cesar Chavez and the Farmworkers Movement.* Houghton Mifflin Harcourt, 2001.

Miller, Debra A. *Dolores Huerta: Labor Leader.*
San Diego, CA: Lucent Books, 2006.

Nahmias, Rick. *The Migrant Project: Contemporary California Farm Workers.*
Albuquerque, NM: University of New Mexico Press, 2008.

Worth, Richard. *Dolores Huerta.*
New York, NY: Chelsea House Publications, 2007.

Online

WEB SITES:
www.doloreshuerta.org/
The Dolores Huerta Foundation connects you with current efforts at organizing farm workers, past successes, information for up-and-coming leaders who want to get involved, and a rich history of Dolores Huerta herself.

www.ufw.org/

This the official page of the United Farm Workers. Here you'll find numerous historical documents and biographies, as well as current news about what's going on with the union, key campaigns, latest news, ways to become a youth activist, and links to other related sites.

www.greatwomen.org/women.php?action=viewone&id=81

From the National Women's Hall of Fame comes this summary page. It gives a snapshot of Dolores's achievements and struggles, and provides links to other significant female leaders.

www.farmworkermovement.us/

This site features primary source essays by the people who started the farm workers movement in the United States in the form of dozens and dozens of first-person accounts of what it was like to be a part of this historic social movement.

www.lasculturas.com/aa/bio/bioDoloresHuerta.htm

A thorough biography of Dolores Huerta, including links to the UFW page and other related resources about Dolores Huerta.

www.nfwsc.org/

This is the National Farm Workers Service Center, founded by César Chávez and Dolores Huerta in the 1960s to provide social programs to support farm workers and their families.

www.mkgandhi.org/

A website dedicated to Mohandas K. Gandhi. Life, biography, teachings, writings, timelines, video clips, books—you name it, it's here!

www.panna.org/

Pesticide Action Network North America works to replace traditional, harmful pesticides with ones that are safer for the environment and for people.

Index

Index

About the Author

In her Grade Two composition scribbler, Alex Van Tol wrote: "I would like to be a book writer when I grow up." She somehow held onto that dream all the way through school and university and ten years of teaching middle school. In 2007 Alex left teaching to write and raise her two small, wild boys. She writes novels and biographies for young adults. In her spare time, she likes to hike, paddle, and hang out at the beach. She is a firm believer in following your dreams.